THE

STERNNESS OF CHRIST'S TEACHING;

AND ITS RELATION TO THE

LAW OF FORGIVENESS.

By the same Author.

THE INFLUENCE OF CHRISTIANITY ON WAR.

AN ESSAY WHICH OBTAINED THE BURNEY PRIZE FOR THE YEAR 1887.

THE

STERNNESS OF CHRIST'S TEACHING;

AND ITS RELATION TO THE

LAW OF FORGIVENESS.

An Essay

WHICH OBTAINED THE NORRISIAN PRIZE
FOR THE YEAR 1888.

BY

J. F. BETHUNE-BAKER, M.A.,

OF PEMBROKE COLLEGE, CAMBRIDGE.

πάθος μάθος.
PAIN IS GAIN.

WIPF & STOCK · Eugene, Oregon

Wipf and Stock Publishers
199 W 8th Ave, Suite 3
Eugene, OR 97401

The Sternness of Christ's Teaching and its Relation to the Law of Forgiveness
An Essay which Obtained the Norrisian Prize for the Year 1888
By Bethune-Baker, J.F.
ISBN 13: 978-1-62564-805-1
Publication date 1/26/2014
Previously published by MacMillan, 1889

TO THE REVEREND

BROOKE FOSS WESTCOTT,

WHOSE NAME WAS ALWAYS BEFORE ME AT SCHOOL,

WHO BECOMES TO ME CONTINUALLY MORE TRULY GREAT AND REVEREND

AS I GROW ABLE TO APPRECIATE FROM A LITTLE LESS DISTANCE

ALL THAT HIS NAME SUGGESTS,

TO WHOM MORE THAN TO ANY OTHER TEACHER I OWE

SUCH UNDERSTANDING OF CHRISTIAN TRUTH AS I HAVE WON,

I REJOICE TO BE ALLOWED

TO INSCRIBE THIS ESSAY.

PREFACE.

THE writer of this essay feels himself largely indebted in his thought upon the subject to the writings of Professor Westcott, Robert Browning, and James Hinton: to all of whom he rejoices to express his gratitude.

He owes much to the careful discussion of the special problem by the author of 'Ecce Homo', though he has not always been able to accept his conclusions.

He has also seen Canon Farrar's sermons on 'Eternal Hope'.

He has throughout adopted an informal discursive method of discussion rather than attempted to compose a formal systematic ethical treatise, believing that such a method will really yield a truer result as being more in accordance with the informal character of Christian teaching. He has tried, however, to mark sufficiently clearly the results reached at each stage of the enquiry, while letting them grow up in natural sequence as the argument progressed.

If there is any originality in the conclusions obtained it can only lie in the particular applications made of thoughts appropriated from others, or in incidental illustrations and the special combination of old ideas.

Through some of these he hopes some little fresh light may perhaps be thrown upon the subject.

CONTENTS.

I. THE LAW OF FORGIVENESS.

II. THE STERNNESS OF CHRIST'S TEACHING.

III. JUSTICE AND MERCY.

IV. THE DISCIPLINE OF PAIN. LOVE.

I.

THE LAW OF FORGIVENESS.

ἕως ἑβδομηκοντάκις ἑπτά.
'Until seventy times seven.'

In determining the significance of the sternness
by which Christ's teaching is in some respects cha-
racterised in its relation to the law of forgiveness—
the revelation of mercy which is so all-pervading an
element in the Gospel view of human and divine
relations—it will be useful to consider first, from the
special instances recorded of Christ's own action and
instruction, the conditions under which forgiveness
is a possibility and a duty.   In the process of
discovering wherein the essence and possibility of
forgiveness consist we may perhaps elicit certain
principles and facts that will assist and guide us
towards the true solution of the difficult problems
suggested by that stern severity which seems to
harmonise so ill with the melodious notes of the
good-tidings of pity and love.

What then is this law of forgiveness, which has *Forgive-*
been described as " Christ's most striking innovation *ness
Christ's*
in morality", and which is undoubtedly generally *greatest*

ethical in-novation; regarded as the most distinctive principle of Christian ethics, so that the phrase a 'Christian' spirit is almost synonymous with a disposition of readiness to forgive an injury?

to be un-limited It must be noted at once that, if certain conditions are satisfied, the teaching of Christ admits of no limitations to this law. " If thy brother trespass against thee seven times a day, and seven times a day turn again to thee, saying, I repent, thou shalt forgive him "[1]—such is the vivid expression of the duty of unlimited forgiveness as taught by Christ. And to the eagerness of Peter, who could not easily at once appropriate so large a principle and would fain have reduced it to the compass of a precise and definite rule, we owe that unmistakeable reiteration of the teaching which raised it far beyond the sphere of mere numerical calculation—" I say not unto you, till seven times, but until seventy times seven."[2]

But although here, as always, Christ refused to enter on the details of the practical application of his spiritual lessons; although in this instance, as in all, the arrow of Christian truth wings its way straight to the very heart and centre of the motive of all action and bears the message Be and Be not, rather than the judaistic rule Do this, Do not do that:—

on condi-tion of repentance of offender; the Master has, however, left on record the condition of the law's fulfilment. "If thy brother turn again to thee, saying, I repent..." this is the condition—true repentance, the sincerity and truth of it shown by the open spontaneous avowal, which implies the

[1] S. Luke xvii. 3, 4.   [2] S. Matt. xviii. 21, 22.

offender's perception of the wrong which he has done and his regret and sorrow for it.

To say that forgiveness was a virtue unknown to *practically a new* the ancient world—the pre-Christian civilisation— *virtue.* would no doubt be untrue and inexact. It must have been a habit largely practised in private life and familiar social intercourse, at least in the small things of every-day experience. But in the larger and more important affairs of conduct and action resentment and revenge were looked upon as no less right than natural and necessary. The pagan ideal of manly life was to succeed in doing as much good to your friends and as much injury to your enemies as possible. The few historical instances of forgiveness which have been recorded met indeed with warm approval from contemporaneous society, but the wonder with which the praise was mingled shows conclusively that such cases were exceptional and that the sentiment prompting them was strange to popular morality and public opinion. The virtue of forgiveness, though admitted and admired, was deemed well-nigh unfeasible. It was not accepted as a working principle in practical life.

Again, repentance for wrong done is entirely a *Repent- ance also* Christian sentiment. Regret for the wrong done on *a new* the ground of the ill-success attendant on it, or for *virtue implying* the suffering which it involved: this every one no *conviction* doubt from time to time must have felt. But this *of sin.* is not repentance; though it may at times be instrumental in effecting that conversion of the mind that constitutes repentance. Through pain and suffering —through such results of actions done in violation

1—2

of the law of nature—we may be brought to that different point of sight from which we see our previous conduct in such different lights and aspects that horror and aversion supersede the ignorant complacence with which hitherto we have regarded it. But if we consider the low standard of morality which was everywhere accepted throughout the old society, in which success was the one criterion of merit, we shall come to the conclusion that regret for the wrong *doing* (as bungling) was doubtless often felt, but seldom or never (except among the few philosophers) regret for the wrong *done* (as evil in itself). Indeed all that even the philosophers for the most part could realise was 'breach of law'; but to break law—not to live ὁμολογουμένως τῇ φύσει— was folly, not sin. Christianity by the enunciation of the belief in a God of righteousness (who was also a loving Father), between whom and man subsisted an organic union—howsoever obscured, enforced impressively the need of personal holiness and the enormity of sin. Henceforth men must abstain from all that might impair that union or estrange the God within them. To break His laws was treachery, unfaithfulness to a personal being, and not a mere infringement of an abstract code. It was, in a word, "sin", and wrong in itself, apart altogether from the results; henceforth it was the *wrong done*—the wrong motive even more than the wrong act—that must be atoned. A conviction of sin— using the phrase in its widest sense—must be established as the *conditio sine qua non* of moral progress; which progress however cannot be actually effected without a new effort of will corresponding to the conviction of sin. It is this conviction of sin that is repentance[1].

If then Christ introduced a new virtue into the world by his inculcation of forgiveness as, in ordinary cases, a plain duty—a natural corollary of the enthusiasm of humanity, it seems that he also demanded from those who were to be the recipients of the benefits of this new virtue a new feeling as the indispensable qualification which they must first possess. *This repentance apparently required by much of Christ's teaching as a conditio sine qua non of forgiveness.*

That repentance is thus closely related to forgiveness is apparent from that one graphic episode in the gospel-narrative, of which S. Peter is the central figure, to which we have already made allusion. And it is still more plainly stated in the teaching of that discourse[2] wherein the Christian is instructed not to remain passive till the offender of his own accord comes to him penitent and begging reconciliation, but on the contrary to adopt all rational means to show him his wrong-doing and to bring home to his consciousness the error and the evil of his conduct, and—should he remain impenitent and obdurate—even to treat him as a heathen or a publican; that is, to regard him henceforth as being outside the pale of Christian life and to have no dealings with him.

And in all the recorded cases in which in his earthly ministry Christ claimed to exercise the power of such remission of sins he seems, as far as we can judge, before he could pronounce his Messianic abso-

[1] *v.* further *infra* p. 60.   [2] S. Matt. xviii. 15 ff.

lution, to have required some proof—such as his sympathetic sense could recognise though others failed—of that condition of soul in the offender to which we give the name 'repentance'.

But also uncondi- tional sub- mission to injuries appar- ently enjoined on Chris- tians.   Side by side, however, with such instances of Christ's own practice and teaching as regards the need of true sincere repentance we find a class of precepts which enforce apparently a different law— the principle of unconditional submission under insults, injuries, and wrongs of the most irritating and humiliating kind.   Foremost among them is the maxim "Whosoever smites thee on the right cheek, turn to him the other also", which seems, in combination with the thrilling utterance "Love your enemies, and pray for them that persecute you", to point to absolute forgiveness as the duty of the Christian, unconditioned and unlimited by any consideration of the aggressor's state of mind before or after the offence.   It is indeed upon such vivid principles as these, which give a special tone to all Christ's teaching, that the sentiment of man has fastened ; the teaching was, upon the whole, so novel that it has not seldom been regarded to the exclusion of the complementary injunctions as to the requirement of repentance, on which however we have seen that Christ in other instances insisted.

Explana- tions of the anti- thetical injunc- tions suggested: And when the difference has been noted, a reason for it has been sought, for instance, in the supposition that in these two classes of cases Christ had in mind different classes of men, and that he enjoined upon his followers different principles of conduct in their dealings, on the one hand with their brother *(1) that they apply respect-ively to conduct to Christians and to non-Chris-tians;* Christians (members of the same society), and on the other hand with those outside the brotherhood, the unbelieving pagan world.

At first sight there is much to support this hypothesis, and all that can be urged in favour of it has been set forth with such authority and argument[1] that it must be considered carefully.

The new Christian society was to be for many years a small minority within the vast and hostile world of paganism—a little insignificant *imperium in imperio*: and it might well appear that very different principles should regulate the conduct of the members of this new society to one another and to strangers who were not in any way committed to their cause or conscious of the claims of their religion, their fuller knowledge of the truth, their high ideal of human life and love.

But on the whole this theory does not promise any satisfactory solution of the seeming difficulty. In the first place, to accept such an interpretation of the different injunctions is to press unduly the word ' brother ', and to regard our Lord as most emphatically sanctioning the principle which underlies the Greek division of the human race into Greek and non-Greek, although reversing the Greek idea of their reciprocal obligations. Such a principle is surely anti-Christian. Not even to the disadvantage of Christians could Christ have inculcated any principle which is, in effect, the negation of the fundamental principle of all his teaching—that *all*

---

[1] *v. Ecce Homo*[18] pp. 285 ff.

men are brothers, that all humanity is one, united in one life, one destiny, one duty and responsibility, however varied its environment may be. With this great truth the proposed interpretation seems to clash[1].

But the most important objection to it—an objection indeed which is quite conclusive—is found in the fact that such an interpretation does not accord with the manner of Christ's presentation of his gospel. It is characteristic of all Christ's teaching that he deals with modes of feeling rather than with methods of working, that he enunciates universal principles and leaves to his disciples their application to special variable circumstances and conditions. It is foreign to his method to command Do *this* in one case, *that* in another. In every case ' Be this ' is what he teaches. It is antagonistic to the spirit of his gospel to ordain one principle of action towards one class of men and another towards a different class. We may not succeed in finding the true explanation of these apparently contradictory maxims, but we must at all events seek it elsewhere.

(2) that they apply to classes differentiated by knowledge. We might indeed be tempted, while rejecting the view just mentioned in its entirety, to accept so much of it as would be represented in the view that Christ—while not distinguishing between two classes of men marked off from one another by external

---

[1] Neither does the contrast of Christ's demeanour to his Jewish persecutors and to Pilate and the Roman soldiers really support this hypothesis. The cases are not parallel (*v.* further note to p. 11).

differences of creed and situation—had regard to
other less-marked differences between men which
would justify and require the adoption of a different
method in relations with them.

There is no doubt that, from a Christian stand- *The ultimate*
point, in the ultimate verdict to be passed upon a *Christian*
man—whether upon a particular act or thought, or *κρίσις has regard to*
upon the sum total of his life and conduct—regard *all differ-*
must be had to all his circumstances and conditions, *ences.*
favourable or adverse to the development and exercise of Christian virtues : ' To whomsoever much is
given, of him shall much be required.'[1] It is a fact,
of which we must never lose sight, that all men do
not start 'fair' in the race of life. Some are penal-
ised so heavily that they can hardly ever hope to
win the prize, and some—if we may keep the meta-
phor—seem to be placed at birth almost within
reach of the goal. The Christian κρίσις recognises
all such differences as these ; and many of the first
in this world's estimation will be last when the distinction takes into account the motive and the effort
in proportion to the power, rather than the mere
amount of work accomplished, the stage in the
attainment actually reached.

> "Not on the vulgar mass
>   Called 'work' must sentence pass,
>   Things done, that took the eye and had the price ;
>   O'er which, from level stand,
>   The low world laid its hand,
>   Found straightway to its mind, could value in a
>   trice :

[1] S. Luke xii. 48.

But all, the world's coarse thumb
And finger failed to plumb,
So passed in making up the main account;
All instincts immature,
All purposes unsure,
That weighed not as his work, yet swelled the man's
  amount:

Thoughts hardly to be packed
Into a narrow act,
Fancies that broke through language and escaped;
All I could never be,
All, men ignored in me,
This, I was worth to God, whose wheel the pitcher
  shaped."[1]

These are Christian truths which we must not forget. "That servant" it is written "which knew his Lord's will, and made not ready, nor did according to his will, shall be beaten with many stripes; but he that knew not, and did things worthy of stripes, shall be beaten with few stripes."[2]

---

[1] Browning: *Rabbi Ben Ezra.*

So *id.*,   "What I aspired to be,
                And was not, comforts me."

cf.   "...Morally, aspire, break bounds. I say
        Endeavour to be good and better still
        And best. Success is nought, endeavour's all."
                            Red Cotton Night-Cap Country.

and   "...'Tis not what man Does which exalts him, but what
        man Would do!"   *Saul.*

v. also *A Grammarian's Funeral, Pacchiarotto* § 21, and the Pope in *The Ring and the Book.*

[2] S. Luke xii. 47. It is this teaching that is the true corrective to the exaggerated view of Christ's severity that is suggested by such passages as that which declares that "from him that hath not shall be taken away even that which he thinketh he hath",

We might thus, remembering this teaching of our Lord, be led to think that he desired us to make a similar distinction in our treatment of our fellow-creatures, and that in the declarations which we are considering he was thinking in the one case of those whose circumstances in life had been such that they must necessarily have known that they were doing wrong, and consciously persisted in it, seeing and approving better things but following the worse; and in the other case of those who—as is said—through no fault of their own but through the force of circumstances 'knew no better'. In the former case repentance was to be exacted as the first condition of forgiveness; that is to say, the wrong must be resented: in the latter case the feeling was to be one of pure pity for the ignorant offender. The distinction of classes would thus be based entirely on the knowledge of good and evil enjoyed by the offenders[1].

and those relating to the parabolic method of instruction "that seeing they may not perceive, and hearing they may not hear... and understand...lest they be saved..." etc. *v.* esp. S. John ix. 41.

[1] The problem of the significance of Christ's cry from the cross, "Father, forgive them, for they know not what they do", bearing most directly as it does upon the view discussed, is perhaps too important to be treated only in a note. The writer cannot regard it—with the author of *Ecce Homo*—as limited in its scope to the Romans, and thus intentionally excluding any reference to the part played in the final tragedy by the scribes and Pharisees and the judaists generally. No one, least of all Christ, could have thought of the soldiers—who were passive instruments, parts of the mere mechanism of social government—as in any true sense needing forgiveness for carrying out what they could only regard as an ordinary criminal execution. He considered even Pilate as comparatively guiltless.   This thrilling cry would

But this idea not present to Christ. His method eternal principles applicable to all cases; not rules for special cases.

But although we may be right in modifying our action in different cases by such considerations, it does not seem that there was present to the mind of Christ any practical distinction of this kind. We may reach a right result by taking the one principle as our guide in the one case, and the other in the other case. But the direct application is our own, not Christ's. To regard it as his is to misunderstand his method. It is to fall into the mistake—so pregnant with peril—of substituting a rule for a principle: it is 'the process by which those high moralities which are the life of the world are converted into the conventionalities which are its bane'. It is just the error into which S. Peter fell. Rules may of course be framed from the Christian principles, and may be useful—even indispensable—as a propaideia to the Christian life. But they never can be the principles themselves; they always are to them as law to grace. There is not one rule in the whole record of Christ's utterances. On the

therefore seem to be rather the supreme expression of the human sympathy and love of Christ. He had emphatically, with burning words the import of which no one ever could mistake, placed upon record for all time his indignation at the sin embodied in the conduct of the Pharisaic party. And now, at the last, almost in the moment of the separation of his soul and body, he seems to separate their human persons from their sin, and, without any change of feeling towards the sin, there bursts from his great human heart the prayer of pure love, the ardent hope for the enlightenment of these blind leaders of the blind. Surely this was a natural and harmonious ending of the human life of one who never resented with a personal feeling any of the wrongs and injuries by which he was throughout assailed. [Cf. *infra*, p. 46, as to the distinction to be made between the person and the sin.]

contrary, they consist essentially of antithetical principles—apparently contradictory, but really complementary one to another, in the union of which alone can Truth be found.

In the instances under review we have thus two principles expressed: the one 'Resent an injury, but forgive it on conditions'; the other 'Waive the rigorous prosecution of your rights'. But we have no instructions as to the practical difficulty of avoiding the violation of one or other principle. The observance of each is not to be based upon a calculation as to which applies to the special case before us. *Both of them apply to every case.* For the reconciliation of them—so far as such a process can be needed—we are thrown back on the resources of our inward spirit, our Christian consciousness. We are prevented from ever quoting 'texts' to hide our failure to assimilate the teaching of our Lord and to appropriate his spirit.

Teaching of the antitheses in combination.

The one command is aimed against self-assertion and pride, and enjoins upon us patience and calm forbearance and endurance under injuries and wrongs: it deals with the spirit in which we should receive and treat them. The other shows us that it is a duty to adopt all means within our power (by argument, persuasion, reason, or even it might be by more forcible measures) to convince the offender of his error and to win him to the cause of truth and brotherly Christian love.

Both of these commands accordingly apply to every case in which a wrong or injury of any kind

The Christian essentially

propa-
gandist,
must
resent evil,
but in
long-
suffering
spirit.

has been done to us by another. The Christian is nothing if not propagandist, and the ultimate aim must always be the reformation of the offender and the triumph of Christian love. But we cannot conceive a case in which it would not be the Christian *ideal*, that is to say an ordinary Christian *duty*, to maintain at the same time a spirit of long suffering and sweet reasonableness—even in the moment of administering a strong rebuke. The two commands together seem in fact to be accordant with the deepest teaching of that well-known motto 'suaviter in modo, fortiter in re'; and there is nothing in the former which at all precludes the necessity of repentance on the part of the aggressor as the condition of his being forgiven. Whether repentance and forgiveness are necessarily always reciprocal; whether forgiveness of a wrong or sin is ever possible until that wrong or sin has been repented of—this is a difficult problem (towards the solution of which we have already gathered some material indications) which for the present we defer to determine.

But so far, having selected for consideration two thoroughly representative antithetical commands of Christ, we have concluded from them the absolute duty of forgiveness in all cases in which the transgressor has sincerely repented of his fault. And incidentally we have elicited the fact that the Christian must not acquiesce in evil, must indeed rebuke it and endeavour to abolish it; even though he must not actively resent the infliction of it on himself.

We may now pass on to see what we learn from other aspects of Christ's teaching.

II.

THE STERNNESS OF CHRIST'S TEACHING.

τοῦτο δεύτερον ἀγαθὸν μετὰ τὸ εἶναι δίκαιον, τὸ γίγνεσθαι καὶ κολα-
ζόμενον διδόναι δίκην. PLATO.

'The next best thing to being just is to become just and by
suffering punishment to be corrected.'

THE very foundation-stone on which any attempt
to exhibit the characteristics of Christ's teaching
must rest is the perception of the fact that it is
absolutely and entirely spiritual in essence. It is
addressed entirely to that element in human nature
which transcends the limitations of earthly existence,
which *is* in the midst of its environment of what
becomes. If we would penetrate into its inmost
significance it is 'by the spirit-sense' that we
'must dive'. The principles which he enunciates
accordingly have no relation to phenomena: we
must not think of them as limited in any way.
No idea of succession enters into them. Time is
entirely a creation of the finite, and cannot be a
measure of the spiritual life. In this immaterial
world—the spiritual sphere wherein Christ moved—

Christ's teaching absolutely spiritual and independent of time and sense.

> "intervals in their succession
> are measured by the living thought alone,
> and grow or wane with its intensity."

There time is not: a thousand years are but as yesterday, and are passed as a watch in the night. Thus essentially spiritual is Christ's teaching, treating of 'eternal' verities which transcend all earthly ideas of time and space. The principles which he revealed and manifested in his life are thus not rightly regarded as conveying to us and embodying everlasting facts, but rather truths that are independent of time—although expressed through the 'forms and images of sense'[1]. Ideas involving the conception of endless duration in time, such notions as 'futurity' or 'past', if found therein, must be interpreted as merely 'images of sense'.

Special instances in the Synoptists: groups of parables. With these facts clearly before us we may proceed to notice a few representative instances of the sternness of Christ's teaching, as recorded in the first three Gospels, and to discover from them, if possible, some general law or principle by which they all are governed. If his teaching is indeed essentially independent of time, we shall evidently gain nothing by attempting to trace any chronological sequence or development in his discourses; and we may well choose for immediate consideration a parable recorded by all three Evangelists among those Temple-discourses which were his latest utterances in public[2]. The most widely received interpretation has always identified 'the wicked husbandmen' with the unfaithful Jews, and

---

[1] *v.* Prof. Westcott's note on ζωὴ αἰώνιος 'life eternal'.—*Epp. S. John.*

[2] S. Matt. xxi., S. Mark xii., S. Luke xx.

regards the parable as showing forth the punishment
to fall upon them for their impious rejection and
murder of the Messiah. But it has also a wider
application. It is declared in it that miserable destruction is to be the doom accomplished upon all
who wilfully and deliberately betray the trust re-
posed in them, and turn deaf ears to the words of
those who seek to win them to a sense of their responsibility[1]. And in the same connection with this
parable, as a corollary to it, all the synoptists add
the metaphorical allusion to " the stone which the
builders rejected ", and all record with slight and
insignificant verbal variations the fearful declaration
of their Master that on whomsoever it should fall it
should scatter him as dust. The exact nature of
this ' winnowing ' it is not easy to determine ; but it
seems certain from the context and the reference to
the image seen by Nebuchadnezzar in his dream
(Dan. ii.) that the disciples understood it as synonymous with miserable and utter destruction.

Then there is the series of parables—of the
Talents, the Pounds and the rebellious Servants, the
unfaithful Servant, and the Marriage of the King's
Son—in which on different faults there is denounced
a punishment of binding hand and foot and relega-

---

[1] Cf. the condemnation of Judas, and the woes denounced on
Chorazin and Bethsaida. In each case the sin is the same—a sin
against light, a neglect of rare opportunities—of the revelation of
purity and goodness in Christ. And so it is said of Judas that it
would have been better for him had he never been born, and that
the doom of the complacent towns upon the shores of the sea of
Galilee should be worse than that of the most profligate cities of
the heathen world.

B.   2

tion to the outer darkness, where is the weeping
and gnashing of teeth.   Of the ill-use of advantages, of carelessness and faithlessness, of disregard of
others' dues—of these and the like sins the issue is
the banishment of the offender from the company of
the good and true to the realm of darkness and
evil.

In yet another group of parables the subject
emphasised is the retributive and agonising punishment that must sometime befal the wicked, and we
have an indication of what the divine vengeance
might be in the action of the unrighteous judge, the
parable of the rich man and Lazarus, recorded by
S. Luke alone, and the parables of the Sheep and the
Goats and the Tares—which are S. Matthew's corresponding contribution to the problem now before
us [1].

In the parable of the rich man and Lazarus it is
declared that no one can pass from one state to the
other, and the picture of the division of the flock by
the Son of Man, at his coming with all his angels,
closes with the departure of the just into life eternal
and of the others into punishment eternal.

The para-
bolic
method :
details
accommo-
dated to
ideas of
hearers.
But with regard to all Christ's parables we must
remember that their imagery was taken from the
current ideas and thoughts and events of the time.
He pointed his teaching by appropriating popular
ideas and applying them to teach the lesson which
he wished to give.   This is the method of the true
teacher, the true reformer, who places himself for

[1] S. Matt. xxv., S. Luke xvi.

the moment as much as possible in the position of *This the* those he has to deal with, and chooses the language *method of* and illustrations which—being familiar to them— *the true* *teacher.* will best impress his meaning, his ideas, upon them ; or at all events so much of his meaning—so much of his ideas—as they are able to receive. This is a fact of such importance for the accurate interpretation of Christ's teaching that we may be excused for dwelling on it, and attempting to exhibit it more clearly by a helpful illustration from Greek art.

It is well known that in planning his stately *ENTASIS* temples the Greek architect always had regard to *in Greek* the position which his work would occupy, to the *architec-* *ture.* angle in which it would present itself to the eye of the beholder. Departures from symmetry are not only suffered, but enjoined, for the sake of a higher symmetrical effect. The straight line of mechanics becomes the curved line of art. In order to correct optical illusions and ensure a perfectly proportionate effect upon the spectator at a dis- tance, the most delicate and subtle refinements were invariably practised. Thus, the upright columns were inclined a little inwards, to overcome the appa- rent tendency of buildings to spread outwards to- wards the top. And again as regards the horizontal lines : because it is the tendency of all long lines to seem to drop about their middle point, the lines of all the horizontal features of the building were curved slightly upwards. Perhaps the simplest form of these devices is that which is technically called the ' entasis ' of the column. The tapered outline of the shaft is not quite straight, as it appears, but slightly curved convexly. If there were no curve, the outline would appear from a distance hollowed. The entasis secures that the right symmetrical effect shall be produced on the observer from the point of view proposed.

Spiritual entasis. It is evident that this principle of architecture can supply us with a lesson for all the relations of life ; in all our actions, all our expressions, all our thoughts, we must consider the point of view of those whom they will influence. In all things we must constantly observe and practise *spiritual entasis.* There is nothing, probably, which will more clearly differentiate the work of the man of true largeness of soul than the mark upon it of this spiritual entasis. And for a teacher it is a primary necessity. We cannot doubt that we must always be prepared to recognise—in our interpretation of Christ's teaching—the operation of this law of " spiritual entasis ". We must not therefore attempt to deduce from the *form* in which the teaching is expressed eternal principles or doctrines. Through the linguistic or pictorial integument we must penetrate to the idea itself, which that particular integument was designed to convey to particular men. We cannot, accordingly, build up arguments upon the mere details of any of the Parables.

This is very notably the case with regard to the lesson to be drawn from the story of Lazarus and the rich man. Just as in the parable of the unjust steward, which precedes it, Christ had taken the maxims of the average shrewd business-man of the world as

the basis of his exhortation to the publicans; so here
he clothes his warnings to the Pharisees in language
specially accommodated to their views of retribution
and the future state.　　And, moreover, apart from
this, we must remember that in all these parables *The κρίσις*
and discourses all that is dealt with is the results of *on this*
cycle of
the human life lived on this earth. The κρίσις *life only.*
thought of is based solely on this cycle of existence,
which is viewed as determining the mode of existence in the stage succeeding. What may be the
issue of that cycle, if it be a cycle, none can tell.

Whether the 'punishment' be corrective or not *Question*
is a question simply not entered on by Christ.　　*whether*
'punish-
Much stress is sometimes laid upon the fact that, *ment' cor-*
rective—
while 'life' *eternal* is often spoken of by him, as the *not entered*
Evangelists report him, no such phrase as 'death *on by*
Christ.
eternal' ever passed his lips[1]: and again that the
word S. Matthew uses to express that 'punishment
eternal' of the wicked, which corresponded to the
'life eternal' of the just, is one which usually means
—in Attic Greek—'corrective' rather than 'retributive' punishment, having regard to the correction
of the offender and not to the satisfaction of the
offended.　　But the word "eternal" might usually
be omitted without Christ's meaning being thereby
affected; and though against a false method of interpretation it may be possible and useful to found
negative arguments on very slender differences of
meaning in the fundamental phraseology, yet we
cannot by any sound criticism attach much *positive*

---

[1] S. Paul, however, speaks of 'eternal destruction' 2 Thess. i. 9.

weight to such a contention: we can only accept it
so far as it falls in and harmonises with the whole
tone of the Gospel teaching.

If we are to cherish the pious opinion that at
some future time all who have misused their opportunities, and failed to realise their life's respon-
sibilities and duties here, and so have been thus
separated from the good and true and have their
portion thus assigned to them with the unfaithful:—
if we may hope that these shall ever win their way
into the presence of the pure and holy, our con-
fidence cannot be grounded on such instances as
these, which we have now reviewed, of the stern
aspects of Christ's teaching. There is no word of
pity, no such hope expressed. The rich man is not
bidden to take comfort in his torments by the promise that the fire which burns his tongue shall be
extinguished when, like the wise physician's cautery,
it has burnt out the fatal ulcer: the crowd that
troops off to the left can see no softening of the
stern determined features of the judge: no gleam of
light falls on the outer darkness.

Thus awful is Christ's teaching in this aspect.
Some time or other all men will have to undergo a
test; and for those who fail beneath it there re-
mains a doom of pain. Classes there may be,
degrees of suffering in Gehenna, as in Heaven there
are many mansions; but compromise there is none.
It is either Gehenna or Heaven.

*But only
one in-*

Nevertheless it is most noteworthy that there
is only one recorded instance of Christ's teaching

that seems positively to preclude the possibility of *stance of* ultimate forgiveness for all men; and this may well *(appa-rently)* perplex students and thinkers more than any other *unpar-donable* ethical problem suggested by the records of the *sin—* Christian gospel.

It is the denunciation of "whosoever speaks *the sin* against the Holy Spirit". Such 'blasphemy' of the *against the Holy* spirit it is declared in one account shall not be *Spirit;* forgiven 'neither in this world nor in that which is to come'[1]. And, again, in the parallel record the expressions are "whosoever blasphemes against the Holy Spirit, hath not forgiveness for ever, but is guilty of an eternal sin"[2].

This, the sternest of all Christ's utterances, fol- *connected* lows on the Pharisaic charge that it was by the *with the* powers of evil that he was enabled to perform his *Pharisees.* works of healing; and it seems that the sin of which the Pharisees and scribes were guilty in making such a charge was specially referred to by our Lord as 'blasphemy against the Holy Spirit'. Nor is it difficult to see its general character, especially as we are aided by the testimony of that exhaustive denunciation of the scribes and Pharisees which Christ, towards the close of his ministry, delivered. It was on them that he poured down almost the only directly personal imprecations which ever fell from his lips. The woes eight times invoked upon them constitute the most tremendous impeachment by which a class was ever stigmatised; they form the extreme instance in Christ's teaching of severity and indignation and resentment.

---

[1] S. Matt. xii. 31—33.   [2] S. Mark iii. 28, 29.

We must endeavour to penetrate to the essence *The nature* of the sin of the scribes and Pharisees.[1]   To be *of the Pharisees'* brief: they were in a position of great authority and *sin.* influence—especially in all religious matters; they were responsible for the maintenance of the Jehovistic belief and the promotion of all moral virtue. That they were legalists and formalists and did not believe in a present divine spirit in men and in the world, but rather in an elaborate system of rules and an abstract code of ethics, was more an intellectual than a moral error.   But what could not be thus condoned was the fact that they were really actors in everything; without sincere convictions, but professing them; elated with the worst kind of all pride—religious pride; thinking themselves superior to all their fellows; and yet mere mountebanks, counterfeiting a divine revelation, and hopelessly deluding and misleading others, even if themselves deluded too.   And thus puffed up with the feeling of their own importance they were jealous of any other teacher; jealous with that professional jealousy which is so utterly contemptible and spiritually fatal.   It was this that prompted them to attempt to excite the passions of the people against Christ by slander and misrepresentation.   They were anxious for their own privileges rather than for truth, and in defence of them were ready to descend to any artifice.   Their sin was thus a conscious attack upon the good and true, a deliberate attempt to advance their own worldly interests under the

[1] *v.* the author of *Ecce Homo*'s masterly analysis of their character.

pretence of furthering the cause of truth and high morality, at the expense of one whom they knew to have a deeper appreciation of goodness and truth than they themselves had.

Some such sin as this it is that Christ denounces with this most impressive force. Having declared that 'all sins' and 'whatsoever blasphemies they shall blaspheme' shall be forgiven to the sons of men, he pointedly contrasts with them this sin against the Holy Spirit which, he says, shall never be forgiven.

If we supplement this teaching by such con- *Some ex-* siderations as we have already noted, we may seem *planation of the* to find an explanation of its unique severity in the *lessons of* possibility that such a sin might so completely *this in-* deaden and destroy the spiritual sense in one who *stance.* had long yielded himself up to its pernicious influence that repentance would become impossible to him.   At the same time, our attention must still be centred round the fact that Christ's teaching, though based upon human conditions, is entirely supra-sensual and independent of time, which is not really a measure of spiritual life or death.

In any case, whatever may be the reason for it, we have to take account of the fact that Christ declares there is a supreme sin for which no man can ever hope to be forgiven; and that that sin is in its nature like the sin of which the opposition to him of the scribes and Pharisees was a sign and indication[1].

[1] Augustine, regarding the sin as deliberate persistence in evil, says that no one can be pronounced guilty of it while life continues

Such in general outline is the vigorous picture that we have from the synoptists of the stern severity with which Christ contemplated the results of sin, and of the images and metaphors by which he sought to bring them home to those who heard him, and to all who should thereafter read their records.

S. John's presentation of Christ's teaching.

From S. John we have of course a very different presentation of the same ideas. Not that it is one whit less stern and rigorous; 'the wrath of God abideth', says S. John, 'on him who disobeyeth the Son'; they that believe not Him 'shall die in their sins'; if a man abide not in Him 'he is cast forth as a branch and is withered: and they gather them and cast them into the fire and they are burned'— like the tares of which S. Matthew tells the parable[1].

His description of the nature of the judgement, as the working out of an absolute law.

But while the synoptists record little more than the fact of this inevitable separation of the evil from the good, S. John describes the nature of the judgement-process, how it is effected and wherein it consists. In his view it is not an act of Christ, but the necessary result of his mission. 'It is not an arbi-

(*v.* passages quoted in Prof. Westcott's *Epp. S. John*, p. 212); but our Lord seems to have regarded the Pharisees as at all events on the verge of falling into such a sin.

S. John's treatment of the 'sin unto death' is an important contribution to the discussion of the possibility of unpardonable sin (*v.* Prof. Westcott, note *ad loc.*).

[1] S. John iii. 36, viii. 24, xv. 6; on the interpretation of which passages *v.* Prof. Westcott: *Gospel of S. John* esp. Introduction pp. xlviii, xlix.

trary sentence, but the working-out of an absolute law.' The revelation of Christ, the gospel which he taught, the ideal of aim and aspiration which he manifested in his life and person—this once presented to a man forces upon him "judgement": in the moment in which this is brought to his consciousness and he decides within himself as to its truth and claim upon him—in that moment he has passed upon himself a judgement unto life or death. By his ability to recognise the majesty and truth of the ideas revealed in Christ he is self-judged.

Such is S. John's interpretation of his Master's teaching. Certain consequences inseparably attend on certain modes of mind: there is no royal road to heaven: the 'eternal distinction' is the unavoidable result of the uniform working of an inexorable law.

It is just this thought which is present to the *Similar to that of* mind of the great Alexandrian father when he says: *Clement* 'For as the mirror is not an evil to an ugly man *of Alexandria* 'because it shews him what like he is; and as the 'physician is not evil to the sick man because he 'tells him of his fever—for the physician is not the 'cause of the fever, but only points out the fever; 'so neither is He, that reproves, ill-disposed towards 'him who is diseased in soul. For he does not put 'the transgressions on him, but only shews the sins 'which are there; in order to turn him away from 'similar practices.'[1]   And to the same effect too *and Irenaeus.* Irenaeus, against those who 'want to make out that God's judgement is not just', shews that the nature

[1] Clement of Alexandria: *Paed.* I. ix. *ad fin.*—Ante-Nicene Christian Library.

of the judgement is as follows: 'As many as observe
'love towards God, to them he affords communion
'with himself; and the communion of God is life
'and light and enjoyment of the goods that have
'their origin in Him. But as many as remove them-
'selves in their own opinions from God, on them he
'brings separation from Him. And separation from
'God is death: and separation from light is dark-
'ness: and separation from God is loss of all the
'goods that have their origin in him. So then they
'who through apostasy have lost these things afore-
'mentioned, inasmuch as they have been deprived
'of all goods, are in a state of absolute punishment:
'not that God himself is punishing them by way of
'guiding discipline ($\pi\rho o\eta\gamma\eta\tau\iota\kappa\hat{\omega}\varsigma$), but that that
'punishment is following on them, by reason of their
'deprivation of all goods. Now the goods that
'spring from God are eternal and endless, and so too
'therefore the deprivation of them is eternal and
'endless[1]. Just as they that have blinded them-
'selves, or been blinded by others, are continuously
'($\delta\iota\eta\nu\epsilon\kappa\hat{\omega}\varsigma$) deprived of the enjoyment of the light
'which is continuous; not that the light brings down
'upon them the retribution of blindness ($\tau\grave{\eta}\nu$ $\tau\iota\mu\omega$-
'$\rho\acute{\iota}a\nu$ $\dot{\epsilon}\nu$ $\tau\upsilon\phi\lambda\acute{\omega}\sigma\epsilon\iota$), but that the darkness itself re-
'veals to them their calamity.'[2]   And so he goes
on to cite the passages which we have noticed from S.
John, and considers that the future distinction of the

---

[1] We have noted already that we cannot really extend such
limitations of 'time' to eternal existence.

[2] Irenaeus: *Contra Haereses* v. 27 ff. (Migne *P. G.* vii. p.
1195 ff.).

good and evil is the natural continuance of their own self-effected distinction in this life.

The sternness of Christ's teaching, thus regarded by S. John and Clement and Irenaeus, is in fact the simple statement of the truth that no one can escape from the results of his own thoughts and feelings and acts. It is no threat of punishment or death to come, but the plain statement that some conditions *are* death; that selfishness is eternal, that is, present death:—a doctrine which at the same time reveals the fact that sacrifice of self is re-creation and redemption, that he that will lose his life shall bring it to a new birth.

In the light of the Johannine inspiration and insight into the eternal we shall have no difficulty in interpreting aright Christ's teaching as recorded by the other three Evangelists.

There is, indeed, one parable related by S. Luke which seems to be the union of the two presentments of the truth. Let us rest our thoughts a moment, in conclusion, on it. It is of course that most familiar of Christ's parables—the parable of the prodigal son. The dominant sin is that which is so constantly denounced by Christ—the sin of wasted powers and neglected opportunities. But on the first proof of repentance—even prompted though it seems by the sense of worldly failure and mere physical hunger—Forgiveness speeds to meet and cheer the offender. This parable is evidently meant to be significant of the relations of mankind as sons to God, the Father, the ideal of

Johannine and Synoptists' views meet in Parable of Prodigal Son.

character; and its special value for us, with a view to the solution of the question now at issue, is that in the parabolic form it shows the real nature of all sin and of its judgement to be such as we have seen S. John declares. Sin has its birth—according to the teaching of our Lord—in the moment when the son desires to leave the father; and separation from the father, which is the sin itself, is thus also the sin's own punishment. The judgement is thus represented as inseparable from the sin itself. There is no way of escape. We cannot violate the laws of physical nature without incurring punishment: and so the violation of the majesty and purity of spiritual laws is itself made to be the avenger of those laws.

III.

JUSTICE AND MERCY.

μεμέρισται ὁ Χριστός ;

'Is Christ divided?'

WE have now collected together the most repre- *Supposed antagonism between justice and mercy.* sentative instances of the sternness of Christ's teach- ing and of his inculcation of the duty of forgiveness, of his "justice" and of his "mercy". We have drawn from these typical examples certain general principles and seen that in some measure they apparently conflict with one another, and, again, that partially they overlap. We now pass on to consider them in combination; and so, if possible, to decide upon their mutual relations and inter- dependence on each other.

The real issue seems to resolve itself into the question of the true connection between the "jus- tice" and the "mercy"—or, using the word in its popular shallow sense, the "love"—of God.

It has been said with impulsive enthusiasm that *The diffi- culty some-* as an answer to dispose at once of all such verbal *times met by laying all stress on love of God* jugglery the one text "God is Love" is absolutely final and complete.

"Love should be absolute love, faith is in fulness or nought."

Now, indeed, it is true that to the grotesque and hopelessly one-sided view of the divine "justice" which has prevailed so widely in, for instance, Calvinistic schools of thought it may possibly be the best corrective to present an equally one-sided view. To the thesis, false by itself, the antithesis—equally false by itself—may perhaps be most effectively opposed. Under the papal system sins could be so easily compounded that a fierce reaction was no doubt inevitable. The complacent—if at first exacting—God of mediaeval Christianity gave way, and in the stead of this 'easy compromiser of offences in return for houses and lands' was reared up the stony image of 'the vindictive father, the arbitrary dispenser of two eternities'. Under this shadow thousands of 'Christians' have been reared for centuries, and so have grown up like the little boy a modern novelist depicts as saying—to a woman who had not been very good to him—'Only think, Euphra! what if, after all, I should find out that God is as kind as you are!' Appalling indeed, and to be combated by almost any fallacy, is the view that makes God less kind than an ordinarily good unselfish man. And it was a truly Christian instinct which made the writer call from the same boy (when much perplexed as to the sins he could not think of, but must needs repent—they told him—if he would escape God's everlasting wrath) a thought

like this: "It always seems to me it would be so
much grander of God to say: 'Come along, never
mind. I'll make you good. I can't wait till you
are good; I love you so much'."[1]   Such a
thought as that is essentially and solely Christian; at
all events as bearing on our own relations with our *and utter*
fellow-men. It is representative of just the fun- *self-sacri-*
damental difference between the Christian and the *fice of*
old religions and philosophies. They were entirely *Christian*
ideal.
and in essence selfish. It has been said with truth
that "whereas the selfishness of modern times exists
"in defiance of morality, in ancient times it was
"approved, sheltered, and even in part enjoined by
"morality...... It was not a mere abuse or corruption
"arising out of the infirmity of human nature, but
"a theory and almost a part of moral philosophy."[2]
In fact, the highest aim of the highest philosophy
was little better than a hot-house culture of self. To
make oneself better was the noblest ideal, to further
the growth of one's own intellectual and moral virtues,
with hardly a thought of attempting to make others
too better and happier.   Against the tendency
to such contemplative seclusion and religious selfishness the whole life of Christ is one grand pro-
test.   Does anyone feel himself superior to others
in purity of motive or in strength of faith, in knowledge or in any Christian virtue?—the obligation is
laid upon him, as a follower of Christ, by no means to
isolate himself in the hope of attaining to a higher
standard of religious life by avoiding any chance of

[1] George Macdonald: *David Elginbrod* p. 329.
[2] *Ecce Homo*[18] p. 151.

contact with a lower life, but rather to endeavour
to seek all opportunities of sharing with others the
advantages that he himself has won, of influencing
for good and helping upwards any that he can.

> "If you loved only what were worth your love,
> Love were clear gain and wholly well for you.
> Make the low nature better by your throes !
> Give earth yourself, go up for gain above."[1]

" Make the low nature better by your throes!"—
this is the truly Christian teaching; this idea it was
reserved for Christ to incarnate.

' Come with us and we will do you good' is certainly the motto for a Christian's life in dealing with
his fellow-men. And it is with reference to the contrary view, in the widest aspects to which we have
alluded, that the great poet[2] to whom we owe so
many a wise and vigorous commentary upon the
deepest principles of Christian ethics has given us
a new interpretation of the old Greek legend of
Ixion, according to which he becomes the personifi-
cation of 'o'erpunished wrong' and the victim of
arbitrary and vindictive power. Bound upon the
wheel in the never-ending torture of its ceaseless
whirl he has long grown conscious that all sin is due
essentially to ignorance, until at last he cries out—
with regard to the arrogant thought, or selfish word
or deed, or human sin and fault of any kind—

> "What were the need but of pitying power to touch and
>   disperse it,
>   Film-work—eye's and ear's—all the distraction of sense?

---

[1] Browning : *James Lee's Wife*.
[2] Browning : *Ixion*.

> How should the soul not see, not hear,—perceive and as
> plainly
> Render in thought, word, deed, back again truth—not
> a lie ? "

And then inspired by this idea, which he feels to be a new revelation of the innate potentialities of human nature, he seems to see the Zeus who is tormenting him dethroned and high above him an influence

> "that turns to a rapture
> Pain—and despair's murk mists blends in a rainbow of
> hope."

And so he rises ' past Zeus to the Potency o'er him '.

Such a line of argument—or should it not rather be called 'emotional appeal'—may no doubt be effectively employed against a popular misapprehension which is almost destructive of Christian truth. It is better to err on this side than on the other ; better to insist on the one fact that the Christian God is Love.

But we have seen that in Christ's teaching all is *But Christ's teaching has also another aspect : the antithesis a true description of it.* not—at first sight—comforting and 'loving' (in the sense in which the word is popularly used). If indeed on the one hand ' there remaineth a rest for the people of God', there is assuredly also a Hell for his enemies—a punishment for wickedness, which is presented to us under the material imagery of burning fire and outer darkness and final separation from the good. The antithesis 'justice and love ' is indeed not Christ's, but it does describe with truth two aspects of Christ's teaching.

Nevertheless, antitheses of this kind, though inevitable, are the cause of great misunderstanding.   It is usually so hard to see that " truth is the union of opposites".

The question illustrated by the Deistic controversy.   The difficulties attending such discussions, and their true solution, are well illustrated from the course of the Deistic controversy of last century.   It must be remembered, then, that it was only some fifty years before the time of this great controversy that the discoveries of Newton had for the first time really brought home to the minds of the men of the modern world the idea of law pervading the universe.   And in this interval three great deductions had been drawn from his discoveries : first, the idea of the world as a huge mechanism working harmoniously, steadily, unchangeably, not with the growth of a flower gradually developing, but with the order of a machine, the same to-day, yesterday, and for-ever ; secondly, the idea that as there was a universal perfect physical law affecting the whole universe, so there was a law of nature affecting all reasonable beings—to detect which law and live according to it, just as the planets steadily unswervingly obeyed the physical law, was the duty and true happiness of man ; and thirdly, the idea of God (as the constructor of the world thus seen as a great mechanism with marvellous adaptation of parts) infinite and perfect, governing all his actions by the same eternal law of reason, with the same unswerving regularity and unchanging purpose, to whom accordingly all 'arbitrary' action was impossible.

It is at once apparent that such ideas as these

might easily appear to militate against the orthodox *Antithesis* belief as to God's absolute omnipotence. And, ac- *—God's will and* cordingly, we find that one of the fundamental points *the law of* at issue between the Deists and their orthodox *perfection.* opponents concerned the true relation between God's will and the law of perfection: was God's omnipotence controlled by law? To this important question Matthew Tindal and William Law give answers that are in appearance opposite and contradictory[1]. Tindal considers that there is a law to which God's actions, no less than men's, must all be conformed. He would indeed believe that God himself first framed this law, which regulates the eternal immutable reasons and relations of things and beings; but he maintained that having given the law God is as much bound to observe it as any of his creatures. William Law, on the other hand, against this view of Tindal, will admit no kind of shadow of limitation to the divine omnipotence and freedom: in his eyes God's one and only rule or reason of action is his own will.

Thus where Tindal recognises law, as limiting the divine action (though in accordance with the divine purpose and the result of the divine will, and even representing that will and purpose to us), his opponent will allow only the will of God as authority or sanction for any action, absolutely uncontrolled and undetermined by anything external to himself, and represents Tindal as introducing an ἀνάγκη

[1] *v.* Tindal: *Christianity as old as the Creation* pub[d]. 1730, esp. chh. ii., iii., vi.; and Law: *The Case of Reason* pub[d]. 1762, esp. ch. i.

independent of any being as the common rule and law of God and man.

The real point of divergence between them is, accordingly, that Law—urging that God must be a being of the highest freedom and independency— would admit God's power of 'willing contrarieties', while denying that his will (inasmuch as it must always have his own perfection) could ever be humour and caprice as among men. And while regarding all goodness as synchronous and commensurate with him, he would yet admit his will as the only criterion of right and wrong.

Tindal's view, on the other hand, is framed in the light of Origen's saying εἰ γὰρ αἰσχρόν τι δρᾷ ὁ θεός, οὐκ ἔστι θεός—if God does any thing base, he is not God.

Law would define 'omnipotence' with Mill as 'the power of doing anything'. Tindal's view is more in accordance with the modern definition of it as 'the power of fulfilling the absolute law of perfection'.

Over the point at issue here the battle was long and fiercely waged. And it is because a battle of identically the same range and character is always being carried on around us, and because the point at issue is exactly analogous to the question immediately under consideration, that we have ventured to seek for a helpful illustration from an ancient controversy. For the difference between the opposing views is ultimately logical and verbal rather than real and inherent: a difference conditioned by the limitations of human reason. If we are to

All such distinctions are logical, not real.

attempt to understand the divine economy—God's action in the world—we are obliged to separate what we conceive as the law of his action from his own being: we posit perfection—the law of his being—outside himself, and regard his will as necessarily harmonious with this perfect law. But clearly this is a logical—a mental—distinction only, a separation and division which has no existence apart from our own thought, but which we are compelled to make by the conditions which we recognise as limitations to our powers of reasoning and intelligence. On the other hand those who take their stand with Law, regarding God and all his ways as necessarily incomprehensible to the finite reason of man, have no need of logical distinctions. Content not even to attempt to understand by the ordinary human processes the workings of God among men, they are able to rest in the verbal and apparently simple answer that the will of God is the only rule or reason of his action.

On which side we are found depends at last upon our constitutional differences; but it is of supreme importance that we should, while taking either view, remember that the difference dividing us is logical, not real; that it is, in short, existent only in our minds, and not in the divine nature. We seize upon some portion of the truth and think we have it all; we make our private canon of the scriptures, like a Marcion or a Luther; we mutilate S. Paul or dub S. James's contribution to the wealth of Christian truth a 'right strawy epistle'; and we set in rigid opposition principles which must be held in com-

bination. And thus it happens that Christ is
divided. And just by the same process comes about
the distinction men have drawn between the justice
and the love of God.

The question further illustrated by the distinctions of the Gnostics, It was this difficulty that made the gnostics
separate the 'just' God of the Old Testament from
the 'good' God of the Christian gospel. And
although the literary victory was won by Irenaeus
and Origen against such views as those of Marcion
and Celsus, the latter really held the field of popular
Christian thought for centuries. We see this only

and by the history of the doctrine of the Atonement. too distinctly if we trace, for instance, through its
various stages the development of the idea of the
atonement, and the later introduction of the thoughts
that centre round the phrase "vicarious satisfaction".
As soon as we leave the language of the Christian
records—their simple imagery and statements anti-
thetically expressed—we see how the human reason,
in its effort to comprehend as much as possible of
the methods of God's redemptive purpose, is compelled to make divisions of the indivisible, and
having framed mere logical conceptions forces them
as attributes upon the godhead. We see how the
human difficulty of always harmonising Christian
love with justice made men practically posit two
antagonistic gods—the one of love, the other as the
instrument of penal justice; and, in due course, how
when the claims of the latter were rejected the
scene of the supposed conflict was transferred to
God's own inward nature, as though within his
mind two principles were always struggling for the

mastery, or oscillating in the effort to effect a balance. Whereas it is impossible for us now to imagine such a conflict.

We cannot recognise in any way the possibility *No such distinctions* of such a dualism. All that we know of the order *tions* of the universe shows us one purpose supreme *really in the divine* through all, one will, one law—a law indeed that *nature:* ultimately crushes with inexorable weight all that *one principle, one* resists it, but nevertheless not until by slighter *perfect law.* penalties attendant upon slighter violations and infringements of its majesty it has afforded all the chance of being disciplined into conformity. And yet at the same time we are enabled to perceive that this all-mastering Power, which seems at times so pitiless, is really always Love; for those who do conform themselves to it grow stronger, nobler, happier than before. It is the well-being of all men —in all their being—that the law is designed to effect; and in the highest interests of all a penalty *The true* must follow its infringement. Indeed in proportion *meaning of a 'perfect'* as the exact observance of the law in the minutest *law.* details of life does really tend to their well-being and positively contribute to the end proposed, in that proportion must the non-observance of it—even in minute particulars—impair and impede the due development of their best selves, their highest qualities and happiness. The more perfectly the law is adapted to its end, the more inevitably must unhappiness and pain and suffering ensue upon the least transgression of it. All is justice, all is love. Violate the law of your being, and Love that has framed the law—so that joy and peace and good of every kind attends upon its due observance—must, or it would cease to be true Love, correct you[1].

Question whether forgiveness is ever possible without repentance.   These thoughts bear directly on the question— the consideration of which we postponed at an earlier point in the discussion—whether forgiveness is ever possible until the offender has repented. If they are true—and they are but a commentary upon S. John's view of the κρίσις—it seems to be impossible that there should be "forgiveness", which must be taken as synonymous with absolute "remission of sins", that has not been preceded by repent-

The motive the one test of action.   ance.   From a Christian standpoint the motive is the one and only touchstone by which action can be tried: the act is nothing, save as the expression of the motive. It is thus easy to see that when once the motive—wrong before—is corrected, and a new and right one substituted for the old and wrong one, then at once the sin may be regarded as 'remitted' and 'forgiveness' has occurred. Others no doubt have suffered by the act, and it has had far-reaching and irremediable results; but those are not to .be imputed to the agent when once his motive is in harmony with the law of his nature.

[1] Cf. the idea of 'propitiation' in the New Testament: the scriptural conception not being that of appeasing one who is angry with a personal feeling against the offender, but of altering the character of that which from without occasions a necessary aliena-tion; the propitiation being made entirely in the matter of the sin (or sinner). But the love of God is the same throughout: he simply *cannot*, in virtue of his very nature, treat sin as if it were not sin. [Prof. Westcott: note on ἱλασμός, *Epp. S. John.*]

But it is certain that Christians have commonly regarded it as a duty to forgive freely those who have injured them, even though they triumph in the injury they have successfully inflicted. It is certain that very many Christians every time they say "as we forgive them that trespass against us"—so far as they are really conscious of a meaning in the words— think of free and frank forgiveness absolutely unconditioned; and this too though no one would place such an interpretation on the corresponding previous clause "Forgive us our trespasses". So that although we all recognise that true contrition for past faults is necessary on our part, before we can presume to ask forgiveness of our Father in Heaven—or even of our fellow-creatures on earth; it does yet appear that many of us accept a different principle as the law by which to determine our own attitude to 'them that trespass against us' under the conviction that the teaching of our Lord requires this of his followers.

Is this a mistake? and if so, are we unconsciously promising what we cannot perform; or is it mere carelessness, so that using the same word in different senses we mean by "forgive" as applied to our own action something not truly analogous to the divine forgiveness, and imply simply that we do not bear active malice against those who have injured us? *What constitutes forgiveness?*

not indifference

In the first place we must remark that it is not a Christian spirit that sometimes prompts the man who thinks it beneath his dignity to resent a wrong. This is the spirit of the μεγαλόψυχος—an ideal of pagan ethics, not an example of Christian character.   Nor again is forgiveness mere impassive *nor pride*

nor apathy.

indifference, though very often it is simulated by it.   An easy-going spirit that is hardly conscious of the wrong or sin committed, and 'puts up' with it just because it does not realise *how* wrong or sinful the thought or feeling or action was—such a tolerant-of-evil spirit is sometimes mistaken for the inspiration of the God of Love.   But the real source of such tolerance is apathy, insensibility, which from a Christian point of view is not only passively un-moral but even actively im-moral.   We learn from Christ that the nature of the sin or wrong must first be felt in all its force.   Unless we feel strongly that there is something to be forgiven, something which is evil—where have we an object on which to exercise this Christian virtue ?   There can be no forgiveness—the word is improperly used and mis-applied—in cases where there has been no conviction of the evil.

Conviction of sin necessary on both sides.   In speaking of the need of repentance we said that a conviction of sin must be established in the offender's mind before he could become a recipient of the healing virtue of forgiveness.

We can now add that a corresponding conviction in the mind of the person wronged is an indis-pensable condition of his becoming a dispenser of this precious balm.

And furthermore we can now perceive that the double sense in which we use the word 'forgiveness' —alike of the agent and of the recipient—misleads us; and that so we sometimes confuse a forgiving spirit, i.e. a readiness to forgive (forgiving-ness), with an act of forgiving-ness—the remission itself (forgiveness). And so we are able to decide that though forgiveness in this active sense may perhaps be possible without repentance on the part of the offender, it certainly is not possible in the passive sense; and that it is thus a mistake to think that any sin can actually be forgiven till the sinner has repented.

At this point the investigation brings us face to face with an almost insuperable difficulty—the tremendous obstacle to a satisfactory solution of the great ethical problem which we have before us; namely, the human impossibility of truly apportioning the responsibility for any individual action. *The difficulty of fairly apportioning responsibility for sin.*

Human life is so complicated. It is so hard to unravel the tangled threads of motives and of causes. Good and evil are so inextricably blended in almost every human act. So often too we may ourselves have contributed, in less or greater measure, to bring about the particular act or series of acts which constitute the offence against us. By omission, if not by commission; by ignorance, if not by negligence; we may have left undone something which we ought to have done, or we may even have done something which we ought not to have done. And the injury inflicted on us by another may be traceable, if only we could see and know its history from its genesis, to some fault of our own which has united with some fault in that other and so in the fulness of time given birth to the particular offence, which at the moment is the only thing *en évidence*—by which alone we can decide upon our verdict as to whose is the responsibility for the particular effect produced.

These considerations, if they are before us in each special case, seem such as would almost inevitably paralyse our feeling of resentment. When we think of all that has gone through countless ages to produce a single thought or act: as the vista opens out before us and our eye begins to range through tendencies and tendencies and tendencies, infinitesimal and innumerable, which must at last have culminated in this special sin; when we consider its ancient ancestry and know that the offender has had all these tendencies transmitted to him—an inalienable heritage—from the dim past, ready to issue into action the first moment that environing conditions should be altogether favourable—can we resent it against him? Almost always there must be extenuating circumstances.

But the Christian is bound to try to do so, And yet, almost insuperable as is the difficulty of duly weighing all the causes and the motives and apportioning the blame, the Christian cannot shrink from doing so. It is certain that the deed, if evil, he must resent; and when he has, to the best of his ability, settled the question as to who is mainly responsible for the immediate result, he must visit his *and to resent the sin accordingly.* resentment upon him until such time as he shall have repented of the act. The phrase "the solidarity of the human race" expresses indeed an awful truth as regards the causation of sin and evil. It is a fearful fact that no man—not the holiest of men—can escape from his due share of this joint responsibility of all mankind. But the consciousness of this

must not deter him from an attempt to grapple with
each special case of evil which may come before him.
The pain which he feels in inflicting the punishment
—the acuteness of which feeling will be the measure
of his own hatred of sin—will be itself his own share
in the punishment, his own contribution to the re-
demption of humanity.

Utterly unchristian, indeed, it is to rush to pluck
the mote from a brother's eye until we have satisfied
ourselves that there is no beam in our own eye.
But still more unchristian is it, when—in spite perhaps of a mote still left in our own eye—we can see
plainly enough the beam in our brother's, to make
no effort to save his endangered sight.   In the discipline of men—the education of the human race— *Men them-*
men have themselves a part to play.   Howsoever *selves the*
instru-
unworthy, they are yet the ministers—the instru- *ments*
ments—of God's supreme economy.   Difficult as *of the*
divine
it is to trace the origin of the evil, we shall not be *discipline.*
excused if we sit with folded hands and view it with
impotent toleration.   We must do our best to extir-
pate it.   Nor, under human conditions, is it feasible
always—or ever entirely—to dissociate the evil from
the person through whose immediate agency it is
manifested.   As Christians we must fight against
the evil *and* its embodiment, whenever the separation of one from the other is not practicable.   The
sins of the fathers *must* in some measure be visited
even by men unto the third and fourth generation.

Of course we know that it may be maintained
that this is for God, not us, to do.   And who would
not gladly be quit of his responsibility by this belief,

to act upon which would make life so much easier?
But it is not so. Our part is the imitation of God
in all his ways, so far as we perceive them.

> "For more is not reserved
> To man, with soul just nerved
> To act tomorrow what he learns today:
> Here, work enough to watch
> The Master work, and catch
> Hints of the proper craft, tricks of the tool's true
> play."

Just as, in ourselves, when we are conscious of them,
we should seek to crush out evil tendencies, so must
we in a spirit of true love in others.   Of course
we may do this in a right way or in a wrong way;
wisely or unwisely: but do it we must. We are
soldiers in the warfare which has for its aim the
establishment of God's kingdom upon earth, and we
must not be prevented from using our arms against
open foes outside the camp because some points in
our armour are weak, and we have often even to
turn our weapons against ourselves.

This is not indeed the method of worldly wisdom; but it is the command of Christ to his disciples. We cannot doubt that his whole life and
conduct is an example for us, in our different position, to transfer to our own circumstances. We
must not take his Pity only as our inspiration; we
must learn the lesson of his Indignation. We must
not cultivate one Christian virtue to the exclusion
of another. In particular cases we may fail, but we
must try: the possibility of failure is not the negation but the promise of ultimate success.

It is ridiculous to cite the saying "judge not, that ye be not judged"[1] as final against such a mass of evidence of very different tone and tenour. We *cannot* escape judgement ourselves by this simple expedient which some imagine Christ commends to us. The maxim has reference to the spirit which must animate and guide our judgement—a spirit of humility and consciousness of our own weaknesses and shortcomings—a spirit that leads us to do to others as we would that they should do unto us, knowing that with what judgement we judge we shall be judged, and with what measure we measure it shall be measured to us.

Furthermore any linguistic argument that can *Divine and* be drawn from the evangelistic records is in favour *human forgiveness* of the view we take. There is nothing to indicate *analogous.* a fundamental difference between the forgiveness which the Christian wins through Christ from God, and that which he in turn bestows upon his 'brothers'. There is one phrase used throughout—a phrase denoting actual "remission" of sin; and it is used by Christ of his own action, and alike of God's and of man's share in the mysterious process. No real difference of spirit or of tenour can be discerned in the various passages in which the idea is dealt with. Everything goes to show that in Christ's mind human forgiveness is exactly analogous to divine forgiveness. Otherwise it would be mockery to offer up the prayer 'Forgive us our trespasses, as we forgive them that trespass against us'. Doubtless in all cases the forgiveness ultimately depends

[1] S. Matt. vii. 1.

upon the law which is supreme over all human laws and actions; but the contention is that it is given to us to remit wrongs committed against ourselves in a manner precisely analogous to that in which, according to Christ's teaching, God remits the wrongs —the sins—committed against Him.

Resentment also analogous. And if the forgiveness of wrong done is thus analogous, assuredly the resentment of it must also be analogous.

And what the 'resentment' of Christ was we have already seen. Our resentment, as his followers, must be framed upon exactly the same principle. We shall thus recognise that while the 'enthusiasm of humanity'—which is the special and peculiar product of Christian teaching—prompts to pity and compassion, and is eager for the development of the highest good and welfare of each human being, it necessarily "creates an intolerant anger against all "who do wrong to human beings, an impatience of "selfish enjoyment, a vindictive enmity to tyrants "and oppressors, a bitterness against sophistry, su- "perstition, self-complacent heartless speculation, an "irreconcileable hostility to every form of imposture, "such as the uninspired, inhuman soul could never "entertain" [1]. And it will be our duty and our privilege to contend against all such unchristian feelings by the most effective means in our power; always with personal humility, but either by quiet persuasion or by open denunciation and indignant expression of anger, according to the special circumstances in each instance. It is in this that we have

[1] *Ecce Homo.*

scope for our practical wisdom, our knowledge of men
and our worldly tact. Christ has supplied the motive
—the only true and right one—and the universal principles of conduct; but the actual mode of working
them out and applying them to all the varied circumstances of human life,—these are details into
which he does not enter.

But the general principles which are to guide us *Summary*
stand out clear and simple. *of the*
Christian
We have endeavoured to 'think round' the *principles*
elicited in
special problem, and so to see it in its true position *the dis-*
in relation to the whole sum of the Christian teach- *cussion.*
ing.   Thus, in the first place, we concluded that
forgiveness of a sin or evil done to one is in all cases
a plain duty on the repentance of the offender; and,
again, that resentment of sin or evil is a duty.   At
an earlier stage in the enquiry we decided that,
resentment of sin being in all cases a Christian duty,
nothing in the circumstances of the sinner should be
allowed to distract our attention from the sin itself
or cloak it from resentment. We rejected the inter-
pretations of Christ's teaching which required us to
assume variant rôles upon the fundamental point.

Similar to these hypotheses is one that we reserved for subsequent consideration: namely, that as
individuals we ought not to resent injuries and sin,
but that as members of society we ought.   We are
now in a position to reject this interpretation also,
as being no less artificial, if more specious, than the
others.   For we may say that with regard to sin
no Christian ever is an individual; he is a member of

4—2

Christ's body. Regarded even merely as a man, he is indissolubly united with his fellow-men in one great corporate existence. And again, resentment of sin is not to be left to governments and social authorities alone, for every Christian is in authority for the extirpation of sin.

And so we are brought, by a gradual process of elimination, to the true interpretation of the difficult antitheses.

It is surely this: first, that sin *cannot* be remitted till it has been repented of; and secondly, that whereas we must indeed always resent the wrong as wrong, we must absolutely never resent it as a wrong against self. It must never be resented as a personal wrong, with a personal feeling against the offender. For him we can have only pity inexhaustible; it is only as being in the particular case the embodiment of the sin or wrong that we can ever resent it upon his person. And even then we must absolutely eliminate from our resentment every thought of self, every personal consideration, and all sense of personal injury.

To resent a wrong with any selfish feeling is to be vindictive, to be Pagan. As Christians it is the evil itself in itself that we must resent and hate :— the evil because it is evil, and not because it causes us—or even others who are dearer to us than ourselves—discomfort, or pain, or loss, or suffering of any kind.

Such is the high ideal Christ's teaching holds before us for our aspiration.

IV.

THE DISCIPLINE OF PAIN.

LOVE.

"learn that the flame of the Everlasting Love
doth burn, ere it transform." NEWMAN.

HAVING now elicited the fundamental characteristics of Christ's teaching in the antithetical aspects of
its justice and its mercy—the law of resentment and
the law of forgiveness—and noted some illustrations
of the difficulties which the great Teacher's method
has presented to his followers in all ages, and the
errors into which they have fallen through the almost
invincible temptation (to which all men are exposed)
to transform the logical conceptions of the human
mind into attributes of the divine nature, and so
transfer the limitations of finite time-bound phenomena to the sphere of infinite eternal entities, it
might seem that our task was done.   But though *Difficulty*
we deny that there are any divisions or conflicting *of recog-*
nising
feelings in the divine nature; though we maintain *different*
its essential unity and declare that infinite per- *results of*
justice and
fection can have but one unchanging purpose and *mercy as*
springing
one unchanging mode of existence and of action, *from one*
and thus that the antithesis 'justice and mercy'— *law.*
while useful as a merely human logical conception

to form a groundwork for rational consideration of some of the problems of human life—is false and misleading if regarded as existing in the divine mind and the cause of different action in different cases :— while we insist upon these truths, we may yet be naturally desirous of understanding, if we can, how it happens that the divine justice and mercy, being essentially the same, act in such apparently different modes in human experience—to judge at least from their immediate visible effects. How is it that the utmost compassion, the deepest sympathy, the most tender and gentlest soothing and consoling, and the infliction of the keenest pain, prolonged suffering, mental and physical anguish—that these can issue from one and the same law ?

This question indeed we cannot altogether answer ; the full solution of the problem, the revelation of this secret—the mystery of pain, it is not given to man to make.

But we can recognise the fact that the ultimate effect is gain, unto life; even though the immediate effect is pain, it may be unto apparent death. To bring out this fact clearly is indeed almost to explain it. So far as the secret can be discovered it is summed up in two words which are the supreme expression of the old-world wisdom—πάθος μάθος, suffering is learning. 'Pain is gain.'

It is this discipline of pain which may be briefly dwelt on with advantage in conclusion[1].

---

[1] Mr Hinton's wonderful essay on "the Mystery of Pain" is, of course, the source of the dominant thought in the following pages.

We have seen that such a thought is never *Pain re-* definitely expressed by Christ; it is Christian only *cognised as dis-* in the sense of being a legitimate deduction from *ciplinary* his teaching, and indeed a fact of human expe- *in design by* rience.   But there is at least one very striking apostolic reference to the fact. "Ye have heard" says S. James "of the patience of Job, brethren, *S. James,* that the Lord is very *pitiful*." S. James here clearly recognises an educational design and end in pain and suffering, and a spiritual progress through it to a higher grade of life.   And this idea of progress through pain was evidently half-formed in the mind of the author of the book of Job, if it had not flashed *and the* upon him with all its enlightening power. He was *author of Job,* groping after it, even if he had not fully seized it yet.   And the same truth had been realised by David in his own experience when he cried[1] "Thy *and* loving correction shall make me great".   In all *David,* the suffering and failure and pain of his life he recognises the chastening hand of Love; he has felt the firm and strengthening touch; he knows that the end of such loving correction is only to purify, to mould to a nobler form, to make him in the best sense of the word 'great'.

But we do not need, after nearly nineteen centuries of Christians have had to learn the lessons of their earthly life, to summon instances to show that men have firmly held that all the trials which assailed them came from a God of Love.   We are rather concerned to exhibit clearly the fact that pain is disciplinary even when apparently merely punitive.

[1] Psalm xviii. 35.

For it seems, if it may be said without disparaging
the saintliness of many a patient sufferer, that often
when pain is borne with most exemplary submission,
it is regarded rather as a mere arbitrary trial of the
subject's Christian faith and patience than—as it
should be—as a distinct indication and teaching
that some law of human nature has been violated,
some principle of life in some way contravened.

It is out of the fulness of his recognition of
this view of pain—as a παιδαγωγός to lead us to
and good—that Clement of Alexandria, in showing
Clement of (against those who think that what is just is not
Alexan- also good) that it is the prerogative of the same
dria. power to be beneficent and to punish justly, says
" How shall we not acknowledge the highest grati-
" tude to the divine Instructor, who is not silent,
" who omits not *those threatenings that point towards*
" *destruction,* but discloses them, and cuts off the
" impulses that tend to them ; and who indoctrinates
" in those counsels which result in the true way of
" living ? " [1]   Thus he describes chastisement as
" the putting of understanding into one " that is the
' bringing one to one's senses '; and elsewhere main-
tains that all punishment is remedial, as wise surgery,
restorative medicines, or careful dieting.   Chastisement dictated by solicitude, he says, is "the medicine
" of the divine love to man, by which the blush of
" modesty breaks forth, and shame at sin super-
" venes......when it is the time to wound the apa-

[1] *Paed.* I. xii.   [Cf. Origen : *con. Cels.* IV. 71 (Migne *P. G.* xi.
p. 1142 ff.), and Augustine : *de vera religione* xv. (Migne *P. L.*
xxxiv. p. 134).]

"thetic soul not mortally but salutarily, *securing*
" *exemption from eternal death by a little pain*".[1]

It is this educational aspect of pain which alone *Pain*
explains its mystery :—the view of it as always the *always educa-*
symptom of a broken law, and thus too always the *tional; a*
great instrument to effect the development of hu- *symptom of disease,*
manity to its perfection.   That this desired result
is effected in individual experience is a truth that
needs no proving.   Invariably the breach of physical
law entails pain on the individual, and broken
spiritual laws always avenge themselves in the like
manner—and not least when the insensibility and
dulness of the offender's nature make him all uncon-
scious of the discipline.[2]

It is not, however, immediately evident that pain *even when*
is educational in this way in those many cases of *vicarious.*
vicarious suffering which baffle and perplex the
human understanding.   For vicarious suffering is no
mere dogma of theology, but a fact of human experience (as indeed are all the 'dogmas' of a true
theology).   Whether we will or no, we *are* bearing
one another's sins.   If we are to recognise a law
of love—or (for the phrase denotes the same) a discipline—in all vicarious pain, we must remember
that the human race is *solidaire*. Each member of
it is inseparably connected with all other members,
and not only receives the heritage—for good and for

[1] *id.* I. viii.

[2] This melancholy fact, and the fact that sometimes pain
hardens and embitters, or even crushes out all sense of good, in
no way militate against the truth that pain is really always a
symptom of diseased humanity—a sign towards the remedy—
without which sign the disease would be unsuspected.

bad—of all who have gone before, but also is im-
measureably benefited by those of his own day
around him. And thus too he has his share of the
evil so-called—the pain—to bear. And, so far as the
human eye can see, the share is not distributed with
equal hand. Where is the education?

True, the individual may not have broken law
himself; but he inherits broken law. According to
the Christian view of individual life he cannot be
permanently sacrificed; but in his person—in the
overwhelming pain he suffers—there is manifested
for the education of the whole race the disease accu-
mulated through long ages (of which his pain is the
index and symptom) which mars their common
humanity, and of which his very suffering (without
which symptom the disease would be all unsuspected)
is the promise of the ultimate cure.   It
is in this way that vicarious suffering—when not for
individual discipline—contributes to the education of
the race, the cure of its diseases, its expansion and
development into its true and perfect life. It is the
symptom, the revelation, of the disease, which must
at least be first acknowledged before ever its cure
can be effected.

*The action
of true and
perfect
Love.*
We have already remarked, in considering the
Johannine presentation of the Christian judgement,
that, if the supreme and ideal law of human life is
perfect, violations of it will necessarily be attended
by results equivalent to what we know as pain. The
truest love has regard to the utmost perfection of
the object of its love, and seeks in every way to

advance it towards the realisation of the ideal of its being. It can therefore by no means permit—so far as lies in its power—deflections from the line of attainment to be pleasurable. That would be to encourage evil and to educate to vice :

"True love works never for the loved one so,
Nor spares skin-surface, smoothening truth away :
Love bids touch truth, endure truth, and embrace
Truth, though, embracing truth, love crush itself.
'Worship not me, but God!' the angels urge:
That is love's grandeur."[1]

It is in this spirit—adopting the personal presentation of the absolute law—that Tertullian puts the question "would you esteem that God good who could encourage man to do evil by attaching impunity to crime?"; and, noting apologetically that we are obliged to speak of things divine by human names, he goes on to declare[2] that it is as foolish to find fault with the means (such as pain) used to establish good as it would be to object to the surgeon's instruments—that cut and burn and amputate—that they are 'mala ministeria', although in fact "without the instruments of his art he cannot be surgeon".

Thus we see that if there were no pain—under existing circumstances—there would be no hope for the progress of the race—for the ultimate conformity of human nature to the likeness of the divine. It has been said that "this world differs from heaven *'Hell' and* and hell in one way ; namely that God's full presence *'Heaven'*

[1] Browning: *Red Cotton Night-Cap Country*.

[2] Tertullian : *con. Marc.* II. xii. (Migne *P. L.* ii. p. 298 ff.).

results of same reve-lation of the good. is not made manifest, but obscurely seen by physical images. The full manifestation constitutes at once heaven to the good, hell to the wicked." [1]   To the soul tainted with evil, a discipline is all-essential; and so it has to undergo a feeling like that which has been depicted as the experience of a human soul in the moment of that ' full manifestation '—

> " the keen sanctity,
> Which with its effluence, like a glory, clothes
> And circles round the Crucified, has seized,
> And scorched, and shrivelled it." [2]

Throughout the poem from which these lines are taken these two kindred ideas—of the revelation of the good as constituting the true κρίσις, and of the discipline of pain as being necessary to the consummation of humanity—find noble expression. His guardian angel tells the disembodied soul

> " thou wilt feel that thou hast sinned,
> As never thou didst feel; and wilt desire
> To shrink away, and hide thee from His sight;
> And yet will have a longing aye to dwell
> Within the beauty of His countenance.
> And these two pains, so counter and so keen,—
> The longing for Him, when thou seest Him not
> The shame of self at thought of seeing Him,—
> Will be thy veriest sharpest purgatory."

In discussing the characteristics of repentance we saw that it consisted really in the recognition of a new ideal, and the perception, consequent upon such a new view, that one's past conduct had been

---

[1] Hinton : *Philosophy and Religion* p. 221.

[2] Newman: *Dream of Gerontius.*

evil.[1]   Such a perception necessarily involves re- *Remorse* morse, is pain. But herein is at once declared the *itself a* educational virtue of pain. For remorse is not ' unto *'rise'.* death ':—selfishness (the essence of all sin) is itself death, and remorse is " a rise, a making alive, and not death ".[2]

Only through this new moral pain could re-demption be effected.   It is therefore with the truest spiritual insight that one has spoken of " the mercy of a minute's fiery purge "; and we can readily perceive how salutary the effects of it might be. In extreme cases of selfishness and sin all human remedies are powerless to produce remorse, repent-ance, of the kind we have in view. We can only wait and look with hope, however tinged with awe, to the sudden surprise of the shock of death and the wonderful revelation that it must bring.[3]

[1] *v. supra* p. 4.

[2] Hinton : *Philosophy and Religion.*

[3] It is this feeling that inspires the Pope's judgement on the chief actor in that great tragedy related in *The Ring and the Book:*

" For the main criminal I have no hope
  Except in such a suddenness of fate.
  I stood at Naples once, a night so dark
  I could have scarce conjectured there was earth
  Anywhere, sky or sea or world at all:
  But the night's black was burst through by a blaze—
  Thunder struck blow on blow, earth groaned and bore,
  Through her whole length of mountain visible:
  There lay the city thick and plain with spires,
  And, like a ghost disshrouded, white the sea.
  So may the truth be flashed out by one blow,
  And Guido see, one instant, and be saved."

But in ordinary cases in every-day experience we see enough to gather the lesson we need.

Recognised failure the condition of progress, the guarantee of success: and pain and suffering the symptom of diseased humanity, crying out for restorative medicine, and thus the certain promise of the discovery of the disease and the ultimate perfection of human nature:—this is the teaching written large on human life.

All limitations really instruments of discipline. Who then would escape such discipline, if he could?

It is sometimes said that it is so hard for those on whom the burden of living falls heavily, and chains and fetters them with galling and painful limitations, to expand in soul-powers and fulfil the high laws of humanity. But really these difficulties are a priceless blessing. The rich and fortunate in this world's estimation, the men who have no exacting calls upon them, no work always pressing to be done; who can choose their occupations for each moment, able to follow their own bent in all things; whose life is a long leisure, with no particular difficulties or troubles to impede the quiet development of the choicest Christian virtues:—who but the thoughtless would envy them?

Let us rather recognise that "to be not disciplined by God Himself, to have to invent one's own disciplines, is a trial under which most men break down"[1]. And so we shall be thankful for the difficulties, the unrelaxing strain and pain, of life.

[1] Archbishop Benson, in *Communings of a Day.* It is for

Let us rejoice, and seize upon the comfort of the thought, that these and all the 'limitations' which throughout this essay we have had before us "are in reality" as one has said[1] "the special application to the individual of that moulding and transforming power, which through some species or other of pain (using the word generically), is developing the sons of God".

It is here that the grounds for joy in life are based amid all its misery and anguish. It is thus that we can understand and thankfully accept Christ's teaching. Perfection the goal to which justice and mercy point: and Pain the path that leads to it : and Love supreme in all and over all.

this reason that the author of *The Ring and the Book* is justified in making the Pope, as Christ's Vicar on earth, condemn the Count with all the more severity. In many ways he had been abundantly blessed by fortune, and not less had he been really blessed in the fact that his path had not been altogether smooth —that Providence had set some limitations to his powers and privileges. He had not been left to invent his own. There were obstacles in seeming set before him: "obstacles in seeming"—but really

> "points that prove
> Advantage for who vaults from low to high
> And makes the stumbling-block a stepping-stone."

And it is just because he failed to make any good use of these 'drawbacks' as we falsely call them—these limitations—of his life that he is judged with special sternness.

[1] *id.* Cf. *Ferishtah's Fancies*, pp. 49, 30: *Easter-Day*

> "happy that I can
> Be crossed and thwarted as a man,
> Not left in God's contempt apart,
> With ghastly smooth life, dead at heart..."